The True Bride

The True Bride

Amy Gerstler

THE LAPIS PRESS · Santa Monica · 1986

ACKNOWLEDGEMENTS

Some work from this book first appeared in the following books and
magazines: *Yonder*, Little Caesar Press; *Christy's Alpine Inn*, Sherwood Press;
White Marriage/Recovery and *Martine's Mouth*, Illuminati; *Early Heaven*,
Ouija Madness Press; *Poetry Loves Poetry*, Momentum Press; *Barney*;
Beyond Baroque MAGAZINE; *Dreamworks*; *Gargoyle*; *Insurgence*; *Little
Caesar*; *Nude Erections*; *OINK!*; *St. Mark's Poetry Project Newsletter*.

*Special thanks to Laura Berringer, Tom Clark, Dennis Cooper, Carol Croland,
Tina Gerstler, Marilyn Okano, Dennis Phillips, Helen Rosenstock, Ed Smith,
David Trinidad, and Benjamin Weissman.*

Cover art by Alexis Smith.

This book is dedicated to the memory of Bert Meyers

Introduction

Sweetheart, I wish you could tour my native land.
...and love me in context.

"Travelogue"

The dramatic voices of these poems are metaphors for states of
the soul seeking its context. They are given existence by a writer
whose most salient gift is her awesome capacity for surrendering
authorial identification with the voicing of the work.

Amy Gerstler's dreams of healing & union are projected into
"selves" – themselves metaphors of her intent, which is no less
than to create a white and blameless paradise wherein our
visions, terrors and desires merge together in the purity of our
imagining them.

On December 17, 1817 the poet John Keats and several
friends went to see a Christmas pantomime at Drury Lane.
Walking back to Hampstead, Keats engaged in a "disquisition"
with his friend Rilke. In the days preceding this conversation
Keats had been thinking much about Shakespeare and the idea
of dramatic voices as masks.

"Several things dove-tailed in my mind," he reported soon
afterwards in a letter to his brother in America, "& at once it
struck me, what quality went to form a Man of Achievement
especially in Literature & which Shakespeare possessed so
enormously – I mean *Negative Capability*, that is when man is
capable of being in uncertainties, Mysteries, doubts, without an
irritable reaching after fact & reason...This pursued through
volumes would perhaps take us no further than this, that with
a great poet the sense of Beauty overcomes every other con-
sideration, or rather obliterates all considerations."

*I should know more about the sky
after all this time on my back…*

"Christine"

"The only means of strengthening one's intellect is to make up one's mind about nothing – to let the mind be a thoroughfare for all thoughts," Keats said in another letter written shortly after the Negative Capability note.

The best test of how much light a poet is directing in his or her poem is whether the beam of his or her attention on his or her chosen subjects also illuminates things around this strangely androgynous space they create, crystallizing and giving shape not only to the subjects themselves but to the whole field of surrounding objects, making those too glow with shared clarity. In opening one cell of reality, the true poet's attention spills over and penetrates the next. This process of overflowing operates all through Amy Gerstler's work.

Tom Clark

The True Bride

Christine

I should know more about the sky
after all this time on my back,
in damp grass, huge moon and gnats
listening, a few whispers stuck in
my throat like fish bones. His kiss
dislodges them and they float up
to pierce the sincere blue firmament,
so mysterious. No ghost of a chance
of getting drunk enough for the
amnesia I need. Tonight's festivities
in this green field are overseen by
fireflies, who I admire: they mate
in thin air and generate light. Good
things they don't sting. I walk home.
Wind whistles in my hoop earrings.
I was lucky not to lose them. A boy
in high school gave me these earrings.
Once in civics class, he touched my
blouse like it was a page he wanted
to turn. For a second, I went trans-
parent, lightheaded: a whiff of
helium or ether, a sheet of tracing
paper or a tea leaf; slight as the
exhalation it takes to say my name.

Since You've Been Gone

Last night, after the satellite shower,
there was a ring around the moon,
the color of ice-dew, ivory, glue, lunacy.
Then a big streak across the sky.
Can you answer questions? What's under
that smeared air? An erased constellation?
Do you look down from your electric chair,
afloat in the charged dark? What are you
doing up there in lullaby land? A census
of blessings? Plotting to come back as
an alligator bag I can hang on my arm?
Choosing your moment to surface through
losses' waters, waves billowing over your
new amphibian skin? Or did you opt to turn
into the wise and bright star I address
this gibberish to, night after night?
Rise and die. Slide down that silver spike
of light. Ignite or untie me. Ah well.
Your intensity's melting and I'm talking
to myself again.

Drifter

To remain in place is a woman's ailment.
What predicament of wind blew me into your lap?
I really wanna know. Housekeeping is a disease.
Its only known antidotes are: fire, flood, train
whistle. The children I left behind sleep
peacefully tonight, tied to their beds,
as their rooms tend to pitch and moan
like small boats mid-ocean. After sex,
the man goes into the bathroom and washes
his hands as thoroughly as a surgeon.
I just lie there.

Night Sweats

Help. I'm trapped in this drenched flesh…
clothes I can't take off. It's embarrassing
not to be able to undress. My silly meat jiggles,
inside this skin stretched on a calcium frame.
On the other hand, it's a privilege
to witness your progress, covering great
distances, and renaming things. Your gaze
is true, as are your bark and bite.
All else seems false and galling. If I
could author a different world, what should
I do? Change myself into a pepper tree
in your back yard? Peek between branches
into your window, to see you blossom
in sleep, absent-minded, leafless and naked.
under the pale cascade of chaff, salt and
chalk dust the sandman heaps over your
snoring head? I just want to watch you live.

Repose

1.

If you slugged me, I'd recover. *Quandaries,*
excuses, cuts, bruises. If you left me
for my best friend, the calm-faced blonde
who doesn't know how pretty she is, I still
might find contentment on the face of
the planet. But if you mumble, lose heart
and throw down all you're holding, I swear:
your bones will not become god's lucky dice
or pave any peaceable kingdom.
Fur and feathers will fly. Whatever numbness, groans,
and seizures my person endures will rattle
your skeleton – whether sunk deep in the
delectable earth feeding ravenous trees,
or burnt to ash for safekeeping, or
hearkening back to carbon at lake bottom.
So you'd better think twice when the time comes.

Repose

11.

If you kill yourself as you threatened,
some spindly red thread will snap as
you make your 12th story leap of faith,
and dizzy passion enters fact. You
selfish bastard. You'd leave me here,
totally exposed, to kowtow to strangers
and kneel at the feet of unforgiving
brick buildings all along our street.
It's spring now so hush up. From the
top floor you can see a billion hapless
seedlings sprout. No need to prove you're
perishable when we'll be hip deep in
wild grass and alfalfa, if we wait. Then
we can wade through it, such a dry green sea.

I Fall to Pieces

What does a kiss mean in our kind of relationship?
A truce of lips? That though we're both animals,
you won't bite? After necking in the cemetery,
I felt scattered as that married couple's ashes.
You read their plaque aloud: TOO BAD, WE HAD FUN.
Hope my crumbs and dust wind up feeding a cactus
whose fruit becomes your tequila. You'd drink me,
and I'd enter your temple: an ever-faithful headache.
But I wouldn't be able to see your Adam's apple jump
when you swallowed. Glug glug. So let's walk upright
awhile, keep paradise at bay, OK? Kiss me again,
breathe your little ills and weird fear into me.
Erase my name, leave me speechless.

Travelogue

Sweetheart, I wish you could tour my native land.
Once you'd seen the dolls in peasant costume,
the unstable terrain, a landslide hanging
by a thread, you'd weather my moods and love me
in context. Even postcards are in limited
edition. You could comb curio shops for years
and never unearth an authentic print
from the ten-cent bin.
I'll unfold my map and go further.
We inhabit only the uppermost floor
of lavishly lit dwellings. Each
apartment is transparent, boasts
picture windows on all sides, no
curtains, so our postures as we
sulk in alcoves, dress, or serve
dessert are decorative, illustrations
for curious passersby.
Often we appear as a congregation of silhouettes,
similar to figures painted on walls of Egyptian tombs.
We cover pages of our datebooks with hieroglyphics,
a historic scrawl that passeth understanding.
Here in the map's upper right hand corner:
an aerial view of the maze which is our
capitol. A shuttle bus can take you even
deeper into the interior, except during
"storm and avalanche danger," the season
I'm most homesick for – to watch the sea
advance to treeline again, as it does once
annually, and flood the dear, tranquilized
landscape, forming lakes in almost every
depression.

White Sleep

Snow is falling all over a poppy field.
Or is it the linoleum? No, opium is growing.
Elephants stumble to their baggy knees
and thud down in the graveyard. Ivory
tusks stick up from the dust like ribs
of wrecked ships. Lucky explorers will
lose their eyesight here, in the teeth
of this gleam. I can't sleep. Thousands
of crickets whirr and cavort in the dark.
Enter the ghost of a man my father's age,
with brilliantined hair, humming a Sinatra
tune: *The Best is Yet to Come*. Who let him
in, with his falsetto promise? How will
the survivors of this night find me? Stuck
full of voodoo pins? Swathed in cotton
wadding, slumped under the train trestle?
Here comes the sandman, who I recognize
by the plowed-under light of his cufflinks —
mother of pearl. My birthstone's opal.
The bed's too soft, Perhaps something more
spartan, a haystack, a furrow? All the lights
in the distant towers go out as the city's
erasure's contemplated on high. Thus we pass
from this world into the next, to regain our
lost natures. Far below: the purple mountain's
crown, the fruited plain, all the sweaters
you ever left on the tether-ball field. My
limp dresses hang in the closet like past
lives without any clout now, starved for

bodies. Let me down you big bear, I'm
allergic to fur. It's not snowing, the
plaster's peeling and little chips are
getting in your hair. Sandman, sandman,
withhold not thy hand from me. Clear the
icicles from my eyes. Blow my composure
asunder, lift the covers, make my sheets
rise in striped rebellion. I've more to ask
but it's getting away from me. So many
incarnations of fathers, dance partners,
whisperers and worshippers waltz by, no time
to describe their faces. Hide where no one
can find you, under the roof rafters, beside
dusty bride dolls, spiders and grandma's
glittering chrome wheelchair: the folded
throne. Welcome home. Set down your suitcase.
No thanks, I'll just lie down in this dark
flowerbed instead, await the friendly
yellow tractor, and bask in the alabaster
buildings' glow as they blink and shine;
the night light of a lifetime. The last
thing on earth I wanted was to go under,
but the unholy loading of this bed grows
whiter and whiter.

This Winter

New gloom. Frozen smoke. Rain every day, with a hint
of snow in it. For once that chump of a weatherman
was right. But I don't care anymore. I flip another
spent Lucky butt to the pavement and watch it sizzle
out. I want it to finish getting dark, quick. Soft
dripping sounds from the clump of blue spruces
across the street. A taxi cuts its light and drifts
into the curb. Stale metallic taste on my tongue
a martini could sweeten. *She* knew how to mix drinks.
I taught her. "Hope I made this right, Mike. Six
to one sounds awfully strong." She called me *sugar
mouth* once when we kissed. Some stupid grin split
my ugly mug for a second, before I remembered why I
never smile. What good am I alive? I'm gutter stuff.
She was something, like the sky, I never saw enough of.
Icy static making her satin robe cling and snap as she
slipped back into it. Her head in my lap, lips glistening,
right up to the minute she became instant history.
Colder now, she's got that head thrown back somewhere,
laughing at me. And the rain's giving birth to a snowflake
here and there. Ah, my doll. Whatta landscape.

January

Funereal umbrellas, black portents
blow open. A far cry from apple blossom
time. A frozen notion clears its throat
to speak and wild, angelic ideals
thrust colors up through the sleet's
crust like ill-timed crocuses. Some-
thing erupts behind my shyness. Was
that your hand I imagined on the back
of my neck, or some prophetic wind,
or a gust of wishful thinking? It's
still raining. O unhappiest and best
of men, who can we accuse? Who isn't
a slave to the unseen inventor of this
iridescence? Be a gentleman, offer
me your coat, I'm cold. I barely exist
in this rapidfire, unreadable wet,
I'm only a drizzle wearing a grey dress.
Taxis backfire and sizzle past. Raise
your eyes to the treetops, above chimneys
and cloud linings, where my presence of
mind has alighted, perhaps that's where
you'll find me.

Chatterbox

How spring comes, 1985 style:
the young light plunges
and tumbles – trips itself up –
ages in a day. Bugs sing.
Babies blink as hair begins
to cover their noggins. Blind
men, in their infinite wisdom,
let themselves be led by
the light that develops out of
events. They whistle Dixie,
clap hands, and the echoes
help them steer clear. How love
sullies one when one wakes up
with it in his eyes. No higher
power than the mockingbird's
sarcasm. She went to sleep
and the next day rescuers
found her alive in the wreckage.
Just think! One more kilometer
and we shall reach the ceiling.

Soft Talk

These may be our last days
to gad about, make calendars
and clutter this planet.
Trees that fed us are bowed
by the weight of an infernal
cloud, and their roots are
shaken. Even with the havoc
we've wreaked since forgetting
we're savages, the blessed
alphabets still exist—
embroidered on pillowcases,
chiseled into headstones.
I read Africa's green, not
entirely photographed. Why
don't we return the reins:
see if the bison and sheep
invent clothes and ulterior
motives when the plough-
horse comes to power. In
Ethiopia, my cousins emerge
from the jungle, bruised
head to toe. On the dark
continent, in mud huts,
and in master bedrooms across
flickering cities, this is how
the haughty men and women
of the earth lay hands on
each other.

Perpetual Honeymoon

Mother promised I wouldn't feel homesick
this trip. She crossed her heart. But her
vows don't matter anymore. My bridegroom
snores on the train. I want him to love
me always. The luggage rack rattles. His
head rocks side to side, looks lifeless,
but I won't panic and wake him. I'll think
about my wedding, those moments I remember:
guests' hair sequined with confetti, my
sweet niece singing hymns, her eyebrows
plucked thin as italics. Then waltzing
couples cleared us a path. The ladies'
jewelry glittered like lights along a pier.
I entered the bridal suite on the stroke
of twelve, draped over my husband's arm,
next to his light suit jacket. There were
foil wrapped chocolates on our pillows.
Not a soul heard me call out, felled by
his soft karate. The phrase "Flight from
Egypt" popped into my head while I focused
my eyes on the whitewashed ceiling. Perhaps
the pastor said it, or I opened the blue
book at bedside to the verse where exiled
Israelites begin forgetting their ancestors.
It's a sad passage. Strange sights stuck
in my mind superimpose themselves over
rustic greenery blurring by: his dilated
eyes at night as he snips my panties with
nail scissors; and a photo of a drowned
girl, her limbs landed gracefully, as if
she'd planned it that way.

Lullaby

Chicken with snow peas sizzles in the oven.
I shuffle down the hall in ragged slippers.
Blessedly, you're asleep. The decals of
leaping lambs and piglets on your dresser
drawers weren't my idea, but your father
feels my idealism's receded past some
point of no return, further than his
hairline. I apologise for his decor.
A flock of plastic birds dangles over
your semi-soft head: (that fontanel a
volcano's mouth) bright ideas you can't
yet collect. They flutter and collide
when you exhale. Only curds and whey
on your mind, conscience clear as jelly.
I peer into your crib's pastel depths
as I'd lean over a well of milk into
which I'd dropped my pocketbook: spilled
its pills, coins, keys, and that old photo
of your father in uniform, looking cartoonish.
I've amnesia about the maternity ward, my
new theory is your father slaved over his
animator's board and drew you, with hair
like wet feathers. When you're older,
I've some extraordinary pictures of Africa
to show you, a glass-bottomed hotel on
stilts over the Serengeti Plain. Impalas
graze, visible through the floor. Leopards
rest in trees. I was into Zen then, cutting
ties with the outer world, but I neglected

a lot of impressive scenery, almost lost
your dad, and there's only one earth, where
water boils, babies are born and the red sun
falls into a drying meadow inhabited by crowned
cranes. Or seems to. Forgive my dolor, my
sweet. We live wonderful days, and I have
the remainder of mine to recover from your
fatal resemblances, my pale hostage,
my little native.

Kindergarten

Why do children burrow in dirt?
To play gardener? Or to escape
their bright clothes and dishes,
decorated with gently-intended
images–squirrels and birds,
meant to keep them safe and
uplifted? Surrounded by carnival
colors that tire their eyes,
sleep at least distances them
from the stink of things breaking
down; the slither and groan of
accidents on long afternoons
when mother lets the cake plate
fall. Raised on Wonder Bread,
children nevertheless aren't fooled
by our bald planet's toupee of
redolent hedges. Regret pinches
them right at bedtime, when they
realize dinners and card games
will go on without them now,
and they taste their as-yet
unexcavated fate, waiting beneath
waving weeds, where animals,
vegetables and minerals trade shapes.

Müttergluck

Some children slip through their mother's clutches.
A stranger offers licorice, or catches your kid
trespassing, and he's gone. *Come out, come out,*
where are you hiding? My boy, this game's gone
far enough. I'll tan your hide when I find you.
Have you gambled away the money your father gave
you? How canst thou come home empty-handed, without
the cow thy parents sent thee to market to sell?
So the child stays away for decades, acquiring
knowledge more useful than any goat, bushel
of beans or basket of pancakes he was robbed of,
or had greedily eaten. Who knows this young man
when he limps back into his village, drunk with new
talents: he can swallow the sea, stretch his neck
for miles, digest anything. Now I see the straw-
berry colored birthmark on this young man's throat—
and though my son remains mute, the little stain
at once recognizes me, and sings out with its
red mouth: Mother Dear, at last I've come home.

Elementary School

List the seas of the world: Adriatic, Baltic,
Caspian. Read the chapter on trees and diseases:
Breadfruit, Leukemia, Elm, Yellow Fever.
Who wrote the encyclopedia we fall asleep
trying to memorize? Filled pages with the vain
names of Hannibal (who had fits) and Charlemagne
(who didn't)? Joan of Arc on her pyre. The sphinx
and her pyramids. Lava beds and tundra. All these
belong to our teacher. She made them up for us.
She's Adam and Eve, authoress of folk songs,
and mother superior to the brood of numerals.
We copy her loopy handwriting, onto wide-ruled
foolscap. She knows which house is ours:
the exact address where our exhausted parents
doze off in front of crises on T.V.
They can't protect us – from our teacher's
crisp, tight-lipped diction, or the brilliant
flash of light the rocket's red glare promises.

V-E Day

Nothing melts our hearts like something artificial:
Television commercials for Jello, the jewel-colored
food of childhood. Pastel sketches of shepherds,
or that painting of Rebecca at the well, expecting
her thirsty future husband to come along any minute.
Radio commentators intone "Victory equals Peace."
Our flaw is eternal thirst for such a belief.
Forty years ago today, the big war ended. Fireworks
cauterized the sky. Speeches were made. Tears closed
our eyes. The gates to the concentration camps were
opened. One liberator married a woman he found inside.
She fell for him because he let her cross the threshold
first, back into the land of manners, sandwiches, and
brave uncles who teetered on crutches with one trouser
leg pinned up. Crops prospered. Graves overflowed
with our ancestors' fossils. The white gauzy shapes
of their ghosts hovered over us, trying to muffle
what was to come.

Berlin

Our grocer's distraught daughter
swallowed a bottle of pills, which failed
to kill her. She dizzily gripped her desktop
to stop the schoolroom from spinning, then
slid into a coma. That night her father
reached past his wife's soft snoring form
to grab the bed's steady iron leg.
At any sudden rumble, workers lie prone
on office floors, sneeze due to dust,
and crack black jokes: "So long, it's been
nice to know you." Widow's city of abandoned
apartments with head dents still in pillows.
A group of sculptors who couldn't shut up
had their works burnt. Is our task to keep
chanting "All's Calm and Bright"; or chatting
underground about how, in certain light,
linden trees and women walking the streets
in tight green skirts left us speechless,
till there's no one alive, above, on German
earth, who remembers such a time?

Impressions of the Midwest

Amidst the knife-bright snows of Christ
which know no seasons, men kneel and weep
for their lost mares and colts. Fate
and the weather are in cahoots–good men
are bested–in this midwest. A famous
window-breaker, crazed by disgrace,
froze or starved to death after living
on ice for awhile. First she shaved
her head. Incest is simple: love
between familiars. With their tongues,
our brother and sister pushed a piece
of hard candy from one to the other's
mouth all night, after they thought
the rest of us kids were asleep. They
died of diphtheria. Yes, it was a sin,
but let's bury them together anyway.
And we did. I remember them standing
stock still in the middle of winter,
holding rigor mortis poses for a family
photo. Behind them, icicles, flashed,
like stabs of envy, from every tree.
Fellow churchgoers, repeat after me:
no one in their right mind has 13 children.

Dry Land

Tonight the coast is clearer than usual,
so we explore the border between wet hysterics
and dry bravery, also known as the shore.
In waterproof shoes, with cameras and tools,
we come seeking evidence of any grain of truth
in the fishwive's tattle and net-menders' gossip;
the local folk wisdom that those slated to die
by fire, for example, wear the firesign written
on their skins all their lives…a blush that never
quite leaves their cheeks, a rash or red mole.
Those with permanently dirty hair or fingernails
will die in a landslide. Those who yawn, sneeze
or sigh more than normal might suffer a long fall,
inhale black gas, or otherwise die by air.
Citizens who slip through thin ice
must have been watermarked.

A man who faked drowning, because he needed
to disappear, camped alone afterwards for several
days on a small island. He fished, looked out
for dangerous snakes, and made sure to obscure
the smoke from his cooking fires. Then he swam
the narrow channel back to the mainland
and attended his own funeral, in disguise.
He saw who did all the sobbing and who
remained dry-eyed. It seemed to him later
he'd seen his neighbors' fates on their faces,
easy to read. One would double up after supper
and be wrapped in a damp pink blanket.

Another would find peace at the bottom of a well.
During a heat wave, a third would put his hand
inside his shirt, and go lie down. They all bore
the brands. The religious also had the blister
of belief in the white lie of an ideal life.
With the first warm rains, and the moon's waning,
drowned bodies often surface. We reach them
as they float home, and haul them in.
We want to look at them. We're curious.
No one makes a show of trying to breathe
into their mouths. We consider
attempts to resuscitate the dead rude
and impious, not to mention messy and disrespectful.
Consider the sour effects on our fresh breaths.
Also, we're afraid of the taste, and what it might
remind us of.

This Explains Everything

Why, humans are drowned before they're born.
Water breaks, and infants gurgle and wail
to clear their lungs. I lost my husband.
His aches, German songs he sang in the bath,
the birthmark on his right thigh; how could I
entrust that to the cold current? And this
speechless grief? Something I meant to ask
him took me too long to say. Now I crumple
his plaid shirt to my face and whisper
into it. I'm told to donate his clothes
to our church's poor. *Cockle shell, oyster,
urchin.* Forever and a day this coast unfurls
a fog that blurs my colorless reluctance.
The sea harbors no dread that keeps it awake
until daylight, crocheting lace. The sea foams
and heaves, doesn't hope some sermon's words
will work a cure on it. Rescue attempts lie
beyond the power of my hands or pen, with
splintered timber. Those who drown are often
surprised by it, in the midst of chores
on board, and so wash ashore twisted into odd
positions. His fingertips, toes and lips
shriveled by long immersion. Late at night,
I remember snores barely escaping his ribs'
prison. I lay awake, wanting to pry him apart,
and reveal the source of that torn, unsettling
sound: his amazing respiration.

Looking at a Medical Text Containing
Color Photos of an Autopsy

Wrestled out of his pale elderly clothes
layer by layer, it's this man's dry silent time.
Once spit made his every word good, if not perfect.
The verve the faithless claim we lose forever
has fled from him. So what's left to do?
Spoon up his body's contents onto ice,
pickle him in formaldehyde,
or lay him out on a bed of wild rice
and try to read his stuffing,
as interns nervously unsculpture him?

With deeper dissection, he begins to look eaten.
Poor slob…a slab with lips, and small ears
filled with grey bristles. His brain an unwise
wad of pasta. The bones of his left hand unfurl
like the delicate ribs of a Japanese fan.
Gall bladder's green leer. A friendly red spleen.
His small intestine impersonates aging sausage;
the heart impersonates expensive steak. Sitting
in your lap, I turn the pages of this atlas,
where the body's shyest territory is explored.
I wish you'd turn your face towards me,
(the mask that hides all your hideous meat)
and kiss me. All my corpuscles and glands
command you to.

Loomings

Like a bride biting off a final thread,
or straddling a threshold, mother's not
lost, she just stepped off some visual
cliff into a more beautiful condition.
Don't say she's dead. Clouds rise up
to heaven. They're vapor. We're skin;
gold in the oven, bread in the furnace.
Something's burning. We wrinkle our noses.
Nothing certain or eternal, she's gone
where there are no noses, no grindstones,
or thirsts or rain during vacation. She
looks like the light from the freezer
at night. Who did she miss, to wander
back like this, beribboned and confused?
When I go, I'll insist on complete
erasure. I'm the right shoulder width
now to wear her furs, but it makes father
nervous. Her work on earth left undone –
I keep finding the notes she kept:
empty ice cube trays, get tin foil, brush
dogs. Open the screen door, father says,
and let that moth out. It's bothering me.
Shoo. Is it she? I know she can't walk
back through the garlic she planted,
yet I sense her presence in that direction.

Slow Boat

This boat is slow, its bow glossing over Lake Como's breathless, echoed blue. Or the Dead Sea, or the Indian Ocean. Who knows? You choose. Where we are is all in our heads. Lie down now. No one wants to hurt you. Least of all me. I desire only the taut horizon, that famished threat of light. Right away. Remember when you almost drowned? Of course you don't. You've blotted it out. Hair plastered to your skull, you lay on the beach, sand stuck to your cheek, making one side of your face look unshaved. The shore rippled and tilted under our feet. Men moved their mouths but I lost the line of sound. Their faces ballooned, each a silent whirling, framed by an intense, wavy heat. There were black holes in the air, as if we were figures in a painting and someone had ripped the canvas in places to reveal gaping darknesses underneath. I never want to feel anything like that again.

Boy, this boat is so slow it seems to be traveling backwards. Flight into the past. A hurricane of girls begging "Let me play with your hair." But today I'm more fascinated by your childhood than mine; the formation of your tastes. Does what I give up for you form an invisible heap at your feet? A pile of sacrifice you trip over in the kitchen? Sorry to leave it lying around. All I never said. Men never kissed to my heart's content. The word "listen"'s a contradiction when written on paper. My diction gets crisper when I tell lies. Your beauty makes me like a fossil sometimes. Encrusted, crumbling. I'm not fixated at any age...I don't have that much homeland or location. This vessel just drifts, I don't row. I'm a stowaway. I just roll in the dirt every day, disturb earthworms, fresh dead insects and live ones that need water to mate. What should I hold against you? Kissing her, then trying to push me downstairs, abetted by gin? What is it about your form, your dripping silhouette, I can't fully remember or forget, without a hypnotist's assistance? Drunk or heavy with love, I must think I'm your lifeguard. It's ridiculous...I can't swim. Last time I fell short. Not enough breath. I want to do it right this time. So I won't have to do it again. My memory of your gestures can never hold a candle to the effect of your presence. How little Spain resembles its depiction on maps. The figurehead on this slow boat peers ahead into reefs and the grey mist of distant weather. She tests the current's temper, then it's past. I'm the foam on the waves, that licks her ever-parted lips. Only I know what she's floating toward or leaving behind.

New Mutiny

Your captain, the man who rules you now, spurts a thousand
pale faces on these blind nights. Because you wore a skirt earlier,
they land in your lap, microscopic droplets with the faces of
able-bodied seamen: cabin boys, cooks, ships' physicians. Push
your damp bangs out of your eyes and try to keep count.
Welcome them aboard this unsteady bed, as …

…the night spirals, like DNA or drunk thoughts. Dizzy
intoxicated stars stayed up half the night to inoculate you. Each
of their five tiny points sharp enough to enter your pores. So
hold still for your amazing vaccination. You can't plead fatigue.
Don't worry, they're sterile, as pretty things often are. Bright
compass points, pinpricks in the firmament, rungs on the
teetery ladder of alchemy, stepping stones to temporary heaven.

The radio's on, very low. A talk show host jokes with his
callers. "I used to have him eating out of my hand" one lady
caller complains. "Now he won't even speak to me." Soon
this man's silence envelops and enters you too. Every object
in his house that isn't nailed down could follow suit, and wind
up inside you. Look at all the stuff you've sucked up already:
measuring tape, a train schedule, that mechanical pencil he
needed. Don't get any bright ideas you're collecting heredity.
You can't pass on what isn't yours to begin with – that's stealing.

The expectant mother's mind wanders while she's crouched
on all fours. Will this rough sex lead to birth defects? One of
these months, she'll prop her infant son up on gumdrop colored
pillows and attempt to explain everything. "A turtle has his
shell," she might begin, "and Mr. Fish his gills. The birdie has
his beak and your pet rabbits their lucky feet. Once your open
head closes, my molten man of steel, you'll become a passionate

narrator or eloquent bonesetter. The keys to the kingdom
jingling in your pocket, you'll start the car. You'll glide out
of the driveway humming music so new its notes wet your lips.
Maybe I'll dry my hands on my apron and wave."
                              (*lullaby*)
    Warm bedded-down lump in a butter colored cradle,
terrified hairless tyrant, distant figure, flash of swimmer's elbows
and head beyond help – past the end of the jetty…why are you
crying? Why can't you sleep? Am I to blame, for eating
unscrubbed vegetables and tainted crabmeat? Did my milk
taste strange, has it given you diphtheria? Lie quiet. I'll sing.
Or I'll read the want ads aloud if that will calm you down.
Lucky you, not to chew or sweat yet. You'll be tall and thin,
with deepset eyes, my plum colored monkey. I know the air's
unbearably still tonight. In winter our yard will look different
under snow's cloak of deliverance. Those are clouds, and this
faint hiss signals the beginning of a light rain. It's good for your
skin. Let's step outside and wait for your eyes, those muddy
unsailed lakes, to focus or close.

White Marriage

1. The keeper's daughter, I grew up in a lighthouse, pale as
an iceberg, surrounded by water, and father's groggy demands.
No mother to teach me to blush. We had a small orchard, in the
midst of a wicked reef, prey to wind, wave and quake. I was
constantly wet, had occasional chest pains, no visitors. Father
laced his oatmeal with cognac that washed up in crates on our
beach. He stayed drunk and silent for days. I was permitted
to walk as far as the sea wall. One sunset, while collecting
mussels for supper, I saw a young couple under the dock. Two
dark postures, heads bent together like animals drinking, or
grazing. The girl's back was against a piling. I thought "Those
barnacles are sharp," but perhaps she didn't feel it. They couldn't
see me. They were busy, feeding. From the pit of my stomach,
a burning sensation radiated out to my limbs, and my joints
went watery. Father had lied to me: that action was no lullaby.
At home, I couldn't stop staring at my father's bald spot.
He was yawning. An aging tattooed man, with little under-
standing of life on dry land. Could I imagine my hair being
smoothed by any other hand? He said, "Come here, Celeste.
You look feverish." He made me lie down. Not even sleep
shields me from the power of his frown.
2. I only hold still for this because you're named for my
favorite angel... the one who protects others with no thought
for himself. One who thirsts for deeper knowledge of me. One
who was raised on a small estate by the river. One who's seen
too much and so bites his tongue, bides his time. One who
recovered from scarlet fever, and ever since understands the
animals' language. One who cultivates plants with sword-
shaped leaves and plots rebellions. One who experiences the

"joy-on-awakening" that field workers feel returning home.
We see them from our bedroom window, shouldering their
picks and rakes, as we spend another Christmas together, locked
in this brothel. I'm sorry I socked you. I know this arrangement
protects me from worse enslavements. You and I were in the
same orphanage, in another life. Don't laugh, I'm psychic.
Stale bread, ugly nuns, and a game we played: queen and slave.
One night you pulled aside my covers, pretending to hold
the royal tent-flap open for me, just as you're doing now. Why,
sometimes, in this palace of strangers, I'm almost homesick
for that miserable place.
3. *Why so quiet, dear?* Just thinking. Remember shortly after
we met, when you put your foot down and decreed: NO MORE
KISSING? I lifted my skirt, so you'd see what you were talking
about going without. But you were right. Who needs that
salad of wilted limbs, followed by a procession of whimpering,
living misgivings? Bless the oak board that divides our bed.
A wave of vapor, really a family of white herons, rises from
the weedy marsh to settle on our evergreen lake. Each evening
they make this short migration, from where they feed to where
they'll sleep. It's comforting to have a routine. Once I ventured
out. A man left his purple mark on my neck, below the
collarbone. Luckily, my husband and I always undress in the
dark, so no explanation was necessary. And the blemish, sin's
grape colored stain, went away.

The True Bride

Elaine sleeps most of the day. She's the prettiest invalid I've
ever seen, and I collect them. Her name means *illumination*,
which I think refers to her skin: luminous and unused as a
newborn's. Her breath smells lofty as an attic with cedar beam
ceiling, ancient papers, forgotten bottles that once held
medicine or scent. Limp Raggedy Ann dolls, and old bath toys.

I've always been attracted to crippled women. I'm convinced
that if they were pruned in early girlhood, the beauty of what
survives (face, neck, hands) is intensified. My potted palm
grows greener and puts forth new shoots after I nip off a few
ailing fronds.

Elaine's legs are all that's wrong with her. Her mother was
rushed one day when Elaine was three, and prepared her salad
carelessly. Germs on the unwashed romaine lettuce gave
Elaine polio. Earmarked her for me. The outdoors are still
myth to her. She doesn't completely believe weather or land-
scape. Phonograph records, stains, telegrams, TV, calendars–
these are her dear flat realities. Her mother tongue. Trees,
golf courses, airplanes, and hail she distrusts as too good
to be true...

She braves perpetual headaches, brought on by harsh and
ruinous daylight. Invalids are experts in bed. Bed and bath are
their habitats. When I stroked her shoulder through her
nightgown for the first time, Elaine was silent for a while. Then
she said "Please go now. I'm praying." I love her odd remarks
and mind, formed in confinement. These days, I move my
hands closer, to sculpt her muscles and she says "oh yes,"
then later, impatient, her hair all unbraided, she says "Hurry
up." Her bed's my pillow-piled shrine. After our long phone

conversations, I know she hangs up a black receiver that's taken on the smell of her unwashed hair, and the receiver feels slightly greasy.

Once I held her hand while she napped. She murmured the word "Africa." Her favorite desert, the Sahara, is a melted margarine color on her Atlas map. *That's why she liked it.* She's exquisite. One piece of zwieback for breakfast. Her luncheon is lemonade. At dinner my true bride sniffs and nibbles my wrist. She insists her strong foreign coffee be bitter, and smiles as she tastes that it is, through her red chapped lips.

She must stand up. We must travel. She'll learn to fry eggs and wear sandals. She'll tan, feel bee stings and slaps. I want to slobber on her neck, then lap her wet hem. Her thirst for suffering quenched, now she's famished for a better destiny.

An army of true brides like her, hobbling women, are crossing a desert. The sand is yellow. They limp and crawl over the dunes, making new ripples and waves on the soft desert floor. They're not afraid of snakes. They're hunting for husbands. Their backpacks are filled with thick sandwiches. Bait. Pyjamas and open robes flutter in the hot breeze. Occasionally one stumbles, loses her shirt, but it's like falling into a pit of raw sugar, it doesn't hurt. She brushes herself off and gets up again. These crippled women don't wear sunglasses, their eyes glint like diamonds. Their gaze could cut glass, or fuse the sand they're knee deep in. I tell Elaine that this dream of so many making a pilgrimage towards us, through her Sahara and mine, a handful of scorching sand sprinkled on a bland map, is my ideal pornography.

Remain Awake

His back is toward me. I'm safe from his gaze. He's naked and asleep. I'm naked and awake. In this round, he's the champion because he's knocked out. I'm the loser, who "came-to" too soon. Since his skin's a healthy color, and he's breathing, I know he's not dead, just in a light sleep, the tail end of a generous faint. Night's almost over, but he remains in the dark, triumphant, still dreaming – of getting bonked on the head by a wild baseball or flying rock. He's dreaming of being spanked by a giantess with a flyswatter. He's dreaming of being drafted into the Marines, and the fly on his blue uniform won't zip closed. In his recurrent dream, he shrinks to the size of an apple seed and gets stepped on. There's a bird with an evil hooked beak in the dream. It blots out the sun for a second with its incredible wingspan.

The knitted quilt has slid halfway to the floor, exposing sheets as dingy as prison issue linen. It's really cold in here. He rolls onto his back. The way his nose pokes up makes his profile look humble and noble at the same time. The sleep of kings. His pores exude a candid and serene scent: a slight sweat. The smell tickles my nostrils, akin to the way in which, if you're thirsty enough, the scent of water can make you salivate. He's senseless. If he'd just stay that way. Perhaps, en route to Africa, he could be stung by a tsetse fly and stricken with sleeping sickness. Then he'd live out his days in a virtuous stupor. I could gaze in his glazed eyes all I liked. I could take his spindly invalid's arm and guide him through crowds, and dangerous deserted places.

The need to eat is a weakness. It irks me that I'll doze again and wake hungry, forgetting my vow to fast down to my sincere marrow. And how did I end up as a full-blown woman, when I clearly remember having a flat chest and wearing my brother's sleeveless undershirts, not so long ago? I don't think I only dreamed it, but these days everything under the sun conquers me: the glasses on the night stand, the shape of the back of some stranger's cranium and what thoughts it might contain, this itching, the glitter-flecked ceiling overhead, and clouds outside. I can't seem to crawl out from under any of it. I don't want to slip back into my dream of children who, with devious sweetness, smash shop windows to hear the satisfying tinkle on impact, then make mosaics in the dirt from the shards.

Seems like my pilot's abandoned ship. One minute there are rumors he's risen... the next, he's down for the count. Quick, how do you steer this thing? I don't want to sleep. I resist being tossed back into the pool where hapless girls in heavy bridal attire drown and thus wed gods. Better to stay an old maid. Five Mayan priests, four virgin soothsayers, three flying wisemen, two witches and one zen master assemble in this unheated bedroom. I want them to write letters of recommendation stating that I may remain awake, peering into this snoring man's ear, trying to divine what looms in the future, without tumbling any farther down this mineshaft, towards tomorrow's well-woven net of words, hot water, and the buttery aroma of French toast neighbors are making for breakfast; or the soft heap I'll be when I hit bottom.

Bread and Butter

Bread is a pillow. Don't you dare lay your head on it. What have you ever done to deserve sustenance?
Eve proved eating is a sin for women.
   In my family, one of the only protests I felt able to make was refusing to eat. To show mother: NO, I WILL NOT SWALLOW THIS, OR DRINK THIS IN. No more umbilical suck. It doesn't flow from her into me and fill me up. I won't chew under her roof. Helpings heap up on my plate, but she will have to scrape them back into the pot. No, dad says he will eat it.
   A stick man was one of the first characters developed in the Chinese alphabet. He is skinny and true. He represents a silence that can be read. His bones poke out and speak for him. He never has to open his mouth, and risk taking something in that will undo, or pollute him.
   Animals who eat from their keepers' hands become tame.
   Here. Your favorite dish. I made it especially for you. You always loved it so much. I only baked it on important occasions. Your name-day cake. Bursting with cream. You were impatient for it to come out of the oven. Couldn't even wait for it to cool. Burnt your mouth. You stutter to this day.
   You have to be quiet. If you can't say something nice, don't say anything at all.
   The truth is hidden in you somewhere. Inside your underwear, beneath your skin, under fatty layers, protected by muscle and cartilage. Pare down till it's revealed. Be severe till it's bared. In a feverish search for sincerity, starve that fever.
   equation: BREAD = LOAF = RELAX = SO YOUR MOUTH FALLS OPEN = EAT WHAT MOTHER HAS KNEADED = WHAT SHE'S BEATEN DOWN WITH HER LITTLE FIST, AND LET RISE AGAIN AND

AGAIN = YOUR INDIVIDUAL SPIRIT, LEAVENED OR AS YET UN-
LEAVENED, therefore, eating her bread = devouring your own
spirit = self-cannibalist.
 If you quit eating, you outwit nature. You become special.
Elevated. Not like everyone else. Your will outstrips your
instincts... you use one to destroy the other. Then you belong
to yourself alone, not the animal kingdom–not the trough
or bird feeder. No one owns you, not god, grocer, butcher,
milkman, baker, farmer, mom or the fry-cook at McDonald's.
What's your mouth full of? Yum! Leave some for me.
The oven, the spaghetti pot, the pitcher, the cereal bowl, the
waffle iron, the pepper mill, the bottomless mug. All yawning
holes you could disappear into.
 The family secrets. Special holiday recipes. Chock-full of
dried fruit. Tales so ripe and difficult to digest, they stick in
your craw. Clog intestines. Once they get into your stomach,
they want to camp out. Live in you. You can hear the stories
you've consumed surge and gurgle, creating wind. You could
explode into a million pieces. So don't even take a bite when it's
served, or you'll never get it out again. When they're not
looking, spit it into your napkin.
 Flesh. Jelly. Sauce. Worms.
 Not in the kitchen. Anywhere but there. Please, mother
I just want to go to my room.

Catherine

A woman lies in bed, half-hearing her refrigerator kick on and hum about every three hours. A book on renaissance art lies open on her blanketed lap. Her neighbor's husband returns home late from a local bar. His station wagon's tires scrunch on their gravel driveway. Otherwise it's a silent night. This woman hopes looking at paintings of smiling calm eyed madonnas will make her sleepy. A black goosenecked lamp has its spotlight trained on the page she's reading. The rest of her bedroom's black. After she finishes a chapter, she marks her place with a piece of Kleenex and puts the book on the night table on top of another volume entitled *Primitive Religions*. Written by a bloodthirsty British scholar, *Primitive Religions* didn't prove sleep-inducing reading last night, with its vivid descriptions of human sacrifice. When she snaps off the lamp she accidentally touches the bulb. She sucks her burnt finger in the dark. Behind her closed eyes tiny red lines pulsate, fade, then re-form an image of the last picture she looked at in the book: a grey marble statue in repose, prone...the tomb effigy of Catherine de Medici. Naked to the waist, the dead noblewoman clutches folds of a sheet or cloth drape over her belly and legs, the way a modest teenager might hug her towel around her in the showers, after gym class. Catherine's flute-hollow bones soften in a copper-lined coffin just under her stone relief. Her head rests on a stone pillow. The renaissance art book belongs to the neighborhood library. Some unknown reader's thumbprint hovers just above Catherine's mouth...a blot that could represent her last breath – or a word balloon containing something she was about to say.

Catherine's modern counterpart shivers and sits up, clicks

the lamp back on. She pulls a quilt from the pile at the foot of her bed and spreads it over her. She thinks of her unhappy grandmother who knitted it. Long gone now, her grandmother surrendered her frown and her marrow. This woman examines her blistered fingertips. She tries not to feel like one in an endless line of granite-faced ladies who lie sleepless on mattresses, sheepskins, or cots–who grimace, try to relax and wait patiently for the ground under their beds to rise like bread, higher and higher, and swallow them up, since they are to be its eventual leavening.

Alice and Lewis

TEN

Once I was, but am no more; his subject, his concern. I was ten
when I met him. He babysat for me. Took me out in a rowboat.
My parents trusted him. Ink sketches, the box camera, his
eyes: he took my picture so many times. Drew me to him.
I wished to be his mistress, whatever that meant: a shepherdess
or milkmaid; the farm girl collecting eggs in her apron,
pictured in my book. I wanted to live in his princedom, the city
he roamed at night. Certain hours only I knew where he was.
I could be trusted. Combing the city for presents for me.
A polished wishbone, a doll's arm, a real glass eye, a fan made of
feathers, my first lost tooth strung on a gold bracelet: an odd
sharp pearl. He had trouble sleeping but didn't mind. Predawn
hours were an alarming blue he liked, so he waded into them
every night. "Blank slate blue," he sighed. "*Tabula rasa* blue"
he repeated, to teach me the latin meaning, "like your eyes."

ELEVEN

For awhile I ate nothing but fruit he left on our doorstep.
Plump black grapes. A crisp crab apple. I'd never seen such
a small apple before. To convey my cravings to him via telep-
athy, one day I strode around my room for an hour chanting
CAKE CAKE CAKE. Later I retrieved a waxy paper bakery bag
from the stoop, containing raisin bread – my name spelled out
on the top crust in raisins. The bread came so close to fulfilling
my mental request that for years raisins and miracles were
linked in my mind. Based on a French expression he'd used,
I constructed my first pun "Lewis is my *raisin d'etre*" I declared
loudly, "my reason for being."

TWELVE

After I had my tonsils out, I hated my parents. They'd given me to unattractive nurses to play with. Women who tucked me into a skinny bed with guardrails. Smiling, they demonstrated on a naked baby doll how doctors would cover my mouth and nose with a cone. When I woke my throat was so raw I couldn't talk. It healed, but I had an excuse to be mute. Proud of her vow of silence, the twelve year old nun scribbled her demands on a pad. Wrote notes to her betrayers: "No, I do not want a baked potato." My mother sent him into my room, with soup on a tray. He balanced the bowl on his knees and blew on it. I loved him so much I had stomach pangs. He began to ask questions. Each response got me one spoonful of hot clear soup. Suddenly I was fumbling for words again, sullen and hungry. His jaw clenched. I could tell he found the sound of my hoarse voice unpleasant. Any second, I thought, he'll be whisked away from me, into another century, to sit on the edge of another little girl's bed. Such was the gibberish of my thinking when I was a child. He led me into the garden, out of my mother's sight. "Those are periwinkles," he told me, christening the held-breath-blue flowers with *his* breath – the most precious fume in the universe, I told myself, oxygen included. My hand in his dry, religious grasp. I was unripe. Twelve. Not yet ready.

Text for Jeff

1. What's all this dark green bad news and refuse? Unfettered, unspoken resentment. All her ill-chosen purchases from local gloveshops; his insolent, irresistible persistence; her inaudible sighs and sea-to-sea silliness; his tattoos; her slim ankles. Do saints hang round the docks like this, associating with low lifes, dangling their feet in the high tide? Once in a blue moon the weight of it makes her accelerate, drive her father's car into a ditch. Advice from on high: don't panic, frolic, resolve or make any quick eager movements. Sit on his lap for only a moment. Enthusiasms, covered wagons, odd, aggressive thoughts. Tears, clash of wills, willows, many aspirins. Unopened letters, obsession with redheads, fever, lowered resistance. Loss of blood, coast obscured by fog – take alternative route: shoals, rocks and breakers gone. This one's thoughts represent the aspirations of the rest of her inarticulate, pent-up breed. Sweet everlasting blankness, kicked-off blankets, idle girl emotes in unswept room; dresses and undresses – film at eleven. Misted vision, shaded eyes. Under the spreading chestnut tree the dismembered maiden acknowledged the accolade, then felt deliciously lightheaded, farsighted.

2. Easy and hopeless, no hankerings, broke a coffee cup, so the moon must be full. Ill luck, hankypanky, loss of purpose, amnesia too. One becomes a symbol then, a placeholder, a cipher that provides light; not a burning bush, but something more feminine and ridiculous: a cookbook accidentally ignited in a kitchen greasefire, which doesn't talk with god's voice or even Betty Crocker's to tell you what to do or how to put it out. Vehemence closes in on her like a packet of snarling wolves.

Add hot water and stir. Cheek to cheek, sea-to-sea, offshore season of giggles, don't waste words or food, what would mother and/or our pious neighbors say? No, you may not leave the table till you've cleaned your plate. Pretty girls like her have armies of suitors to wade through, all with similar IQs. On the other hand, the very sight of him trying to cross the street: his funny run, ironclad weaknesses, hypochondria, squinting at street signs, wincing as he gets splattered by what runs out of a rain gutter...why kiss such a clod? He's got chipped teeth, he's mean to mother, all he eats is potatoes, and you keep trying to maneuver him under the mistletoe–your hormones must be misfiring. Briefly contemplate your other available fates. This one's not sealed. No cure yet for the persistence of vision. So dry your eyes.

3. I'm innocent, though typhus virus and tragedy swirls and eddies around me like invincible weather. Emotional climate becomes unbreathable earthly routine. The usual mundane satellites stick to their orbits, moss and shrubs continue flowering. Someone unheroic takes a bite out of your arm or hamburger, but it's gauche to slap a man these days so there's nothing you can do about it. Give up English, learn German. Come, grief, and tower over me, it's spring. It's spring, and books are written, their authors quizzical or depressed, but the grunion aren't running. "Unendurable daylight," screams the man with the migraine, less immune than ever. You can write with the smoothest writing quality pencil ever made and still have nada to say. You can take tranquilizers like the rest of your empty headed gender. If you don't eat enough leafy greens you'll feel slighted all the time, become so over-sensitive to light

you'll be blinded by the sight of mother of pearl. If you lose
your necklace again and force your gullible fiance to go down
on his hands and knees and crawl around searching for it, you've
good reason to feel guilty and foolish for wearing Woolworth's
jewelry in the first place. Just follow your instincts or revise
your diet. That'll clear those glazed peepers.

4. There's the ledger lying open on the lush blue rug that
resembles the deep blue sea. His haggard face hovers above the
want ads. Who needs trained waitresses this time of year?
I can stay on my feet a long time. Ships could sink, deluges
swallow museums, lawyers snow juries, but I swear as long as I
still have my eyesight, I may blink and get reluctant a lot,
become whiny and damp but I'll never leave you in the lurch.
Trying to find it by moonlight. Ideas elusive as helium.
Better left unsaid. Elope with a rope ladder. She's not dumb,
just uncultivated. Try being nice to her. Or send her to college.
Do you think the maid overheard us? Oh no. The whole
house seemed to tilt, and things fell off shelves. Too bad you
weren't here. Quite a sight: broken lamps and brownish water
damage. All your sins summed up on one page. Misspelled
complaints will be disregarded. Remember, we're perfectionists
up here. We see everything.

5. Then there was the matter of his moodiness, his "blackness,"
the abyss his system was based on; which entered her blood-
stream, much as a drug does. A chasm exists even between
sympathetics. It's thrilling to see real darkness again, though,
out beyond the reach of yellow undertow: the domestic net
cast by the light of living room lamps. One day you wake

grown. You grimace, ruled by hairiness and hormones, form filled out–you find yourself expected to walk upright, have manners, and wear clothes. Your wife's panties, her holiest pair, a talisman, devoutly stuffed into your back pocket to keep you safe from harm. Naturally, you want to run howling back to the woods you left. But viewed through the kitchen window, the forest appears irreparably mangy now. Dinner's on the stove. The dogs whine to be let in. Mother had such a lucid gaze in those old photos. What were her eyes fixed on all that time? Her elusive, sacred duty? Finish your milk. No, young lady, you may not leave the table until you've cleaned your plate. You seemed unmoved when I got so emotional on the phone. Here's my biography, from birth till now. 778 pages: an easy read. No, no; go ahead, finish your eggs and kippers first, don't try to read while you're eating, it'll keep. He knew nothing of her checkered past... was unaware that, like Poland, she'd been "taken over" many times. You can assemble a narrative out of the stains on the ceiling, the mothballs in the front hall closet, the leftover romaine and tomatoes swimming in oil. So many fruitless endeavors. Can you use this or should I throw it away? Try this mossy poison to undermine your misery; climb this rickety, flower ridden trellis. Ease between these lackluster sheets. Swallow this ball of sleep balm, made of poppy seeds. O open your mouth and close your eyes.

Martine's Mouth

The moment I first glimpsed Martine's mouth, I knew there was going to be trouble, of a sexual, complicated nature. Vlad, who I had driven to the bowling alley with, noticed too. It's great watching Vlad fight to keep a straight face. I guess he thinks that mustache helps. Oh well. Martine had a little swaying curtain of red-gold jaw length hair. Blunt cut, straight as iron. It swung in front of and away from her cake-white face, concealing and revealing her alternating current: shy boy/cool aggressive chick. It barely held the light with its burnish, but snagged my eye, so I didn't focus in on her mouth right away. But then she moved, the hair swung open again, and she wetted her lips to ask for a cigarette. I doubt my face gave any indication of what I was feeling. I'm famous for blankness, being Mr. Impassivity, especially when dumbstruck. But the sight of Martine's mouth sounded a subterranean chord in my softest, innermost organs. Maybe something like the semi-pleasant visceral twinge I've heard women claim grabs them at ovulation. My guts screeched to a halt…quit secreting, to listen. It seemed the whole bowling alley shut up. Martine's mouth poised on the brim of a first syllable. "*What's your name again?*" My belly clenched for a second. I closed my eyes. She spoke. Then it was over. I opened them. A few more airless seconds passed. One of those creatures who hardly ever per-spires, I was instantly wearing one of those prickly thin acidic sweats, citrus-y smelling as piss. The bowling alley colored itself in again, started to look more normal. Martine's beer arrived. I watched her sip it. I had no cigarettes. The strange elevation, the no-need-to-breathe sensation faded. I ordered a shot from the roving waitress, to make sure I'd revived. Until it arrived, the shattering sound of pins being knocked down helped clear my head. I drank and watched Martine's mouth for the next quarter hour, pretending to be seeing various oriental couples eat shrimp chips and throw graceful accurate strikes. I had to keep blinking a lot. My eyes were drying out. Staring. The whole night seemed like a stop action film. Martine's mouth, raised from the plane of her face: a bit of dangerous braille. Her mouth made me feel soft and hard, torn and poked, calm and terrorized, bland and overexcited. I crossed my legs. Still, she sat and chatted below on the lane, her mouth stuck out, an impossible cactus blossom that looked slightly un-natural—grafted on where it bloomed.

Why did her mouth make me remember things? For no reason at all, when I saw Martine's mouth, I thought of an August vacation, on the shore of a Florida lake. A girl came running up a white sand beach toward where I was lying. Ada, daughter of a painter friend of my father's. She leaned over, panting, to drip on me, blocking the light. Her bathing suit had but one strap. I told her it made her look like Tarzan. She ran off to feed the Canadian geese. Their wings had been clipped by her father, the lake owner, so he could sketch the geese without their flying away. A clear liquid leaked from the cut ends of some of the bigger feathers the wind had scattered on the grass and sand. I never knew there was fluid in the shafts of those feathers. We were ten and eleven. Maybe the connection is Ada's bathing suit. *Fuschia*. Martine's mouth always made me think of hothouse plants. Her mouth looked like something grown indoors, not quite ripe. Just my cup of tea. Her lips on the rim, tipping the hot liquid toward her lovely gullet.

Her eyes were unremarkable, although wide. The color of

glassy algae. I'd as soon, I told her once in a foul mood, gaze into a plate of noodles. But I was hot to look down her throat. How many nights did I lie on my back wondering what the roof of her mouth looked like? A wrinkled red lid? And the far side of her even teeth? (She'd worn braces for eight years.) And her thick moist tongue, tongue of some patient ruminator – a cow or doe at a salt lick. The tongue covered by whitish tastebuds like the velvet nap on elks' antlers. Once when she thought she had tonsilitis, I had my big chance. I insisted on fetching a flashlight and looking into her throat. It interested me more than her cunt. I can't explain. One hand gently behind her head to steady her, the other training light down the tunnel. More sincere, less oppressed noises came rumbling up from that cavern than squeaked out of her lower half. The gleam of her teeth was a real lure: bone-glow in oral dark. I felt like Tom Sawyer lost in the exhilarating cave with Becky Thatcher, having strayed from the rest of the picnickers; writing their names in the clammy walls in candle smoke. I'd love to have left my mark on Martine's gum, or the soft tissue lining her mouth. My name *there*, pricked into a tattoo: I WAS HERE BEFORE YOU, for later intruders to taste, read, ignore or shrug off.

A Lecture on Jealousy

Jealousy can be smelled, if you've a nose for it, like mildew,
garlic, or the fear-scented sweat rabid dogs find humans to bite
by. Jealousy makes pastry taste bad, hobbles your gait, causes
your right hand to write checks for sums your left hand never
had. Jealousy can make sufferers hate harmless objects. Match-
books, letters, eyebrow pencils – innocuous props we all need
to fidget with, become EVIDENCE. The only known cure for
this wasting disease is to cultivate a love for your rival. Earnest,
passionate admiration, with all the tremblings and trimmings.
Sleepless nights spent wondering "What does she have that
I don't have/What does she leak that I've run dry of?" must be
given over to serious research. Her white neck, her slender
wrists, her great taste in A-line skirts, her confusion at stoplights,
her old hands and young feet, her perfume – or is it coconut
soap, the deft motion with which she flicks cigarette ashes
hither and yon, her loud red blouse, her love of cherry tomatoes,
her sneeze, her eggs benedict, her secrecy, the drone of her hair
dryer, the amazing way she always looks like she's had her hair
cut yesterday...see how easy it is? Her drug problem, her
insomnia, her dress size, her polka-dot bikini, her pony skin
wallet, her saliva which tastes so great...for god's sake, some-
body stop me.

Dear Boy George

Only three things on earth seem useful or soothing to me.
One: wearing stolen clothes. Two: photos of exquisitely
dressed redheads. Three: your voice on the radio. Those songs
fall smack-dab into my range! Not to embarrass you with my
raw American awe, or let you think I'm the kinda girl who
bends over for any guy who plucks his eyebrows and can make
tight braids – but you're the plump bisexual cherub of the
eighties: clusters of Rubens' painted angels, plus a dollop of the
Pillsbury dough boy, all rolled into one! We could go skating,
or just lie around my house eating pineapple. I could pierce
your ears: I know how to freeze the lobes with ice so it doesn't
hurt. When I misunderstand your lyrics, they get even better.
I thought the line I'M YOUR LOVER, NOT YOUR RIVAL, was I'M
ANOTHER, NOT THE BIBLE, or PRIME YOUR MOTHER, NOT A LIBEL,
or UNDERCOVER BOUGHT ARRIVAL. Great, huh? See, we're of like
minds. I almost died when I read in the *Times* how you saved
that girl from drowning ... dived down and pulled the blub-
bering sissy up. I'd give anything to be the limp, dripping
form you stumbled from the lake with, draped over your pale,
motherly arms, in a grateful faint, as your mascara ran and ran.

A Letter

Dear Uncle,

I'm lying on a Japanese mat, pretending to tan, on vacation on this island you recommended to mother. Don't worry, I'm keeping an eye on my delicate skin. Wish I could say the same for my escort. He's sulky, says this dry heat makes him depressed. I fished the keys out of my purse for him just now, and he stalked off. He'll either go back to his sombre German novel or that too-well-lit tourist bar. He's a young artist, and you know how they suffer, being a hopeless intellectual yourself. At least you had the sense to marry aunt Andrea, and she did a better job on you than anyone expected. Actually, this latest boyfriend of mine looks a lot like you. That's why I picked him. How could you write me all that nonsense last summer about age differences, unselfish love, and the purity of yearning? It made me furious. I decided you were either cruel or trying to drive me crazy. Yearning is NEVER purer than consummation. I'm certain of this, as an uncivilised sun beats down on my salty hair. None of us, even in our aberrant family, will live forever. The only satisfaction available in this world is in what you can lay your hands on...not what you have to gaze at from afar with virtuous restraint, or what you must recreate, night after sleepless night, to feed an inflamed imagination. I've had a crush on you since I was eleven. My parents and I were at a barbeque at your house. You made steaks. After dinner, you collected my limp, stained paper plate, and your hand brushed my bare leg. That night I felt funny and couldn't sleep. I had goosebumps. Now I want an encore. I'm getting burnt, better sign off. If you're as smart as you're supposed to be, you'll think about this and realize I'm right.

Yours,
Emily

Molly

It wasn't our fault. We plead innocent. She was a strange looking baby, but we didn't think it would help our daughter in later life to give her an oddball name. Molly seemed a soft enough moniker. A pink sweet in the mouth. We hoped she'd live up to it. Our little girl, graced with a name chewy as marzipan. Plump. Comforting. A chocolate-covered cherry that oozes sugar-liquor. We simply mischristened her. Parents beware. We would have done better to have taken a hard look at our offspring, and not choose a name that contradicted her personality. We should have called her Clem, Ash, Erzulie, Placenta, Machete, Nono, Aorta, Myopia.

She was born so nearsighted that she needed glasses immediately. We rushed Molly to the eye doctor. That was another mistake…assuming she *wanted* to be able to see. We should have named her something difficult, squinty and thin. A name should serve as a veil, or in our poor Molly's case as a cloak of invisibility.

Dear Molly, we were so naive. Just a couple of wide-eyed kids in love. Your parents, wanting to populate the world with a race of incarnations of each other. We thought your name sounded hearty. Irish. A soprano's stage name. But Molly isn't interested in singing.

The capital M, a slanted roof whose two points jab into and irritate the sky. The o's a tiny window. The twin l's represent a rungless ladder leaned against the house. Lightning struck the man who was climbing it to repair the roof. The forked y is a lie. Its tail dangles like a thread of drool from the mouth, so the speaker is left with their tongue hanging out at the last vowel.

It goes without saying that our Molly is an only child.
Our baby turned out to be gay. Of course that could change.
She's still young, and these days there's all kinds of help
available for those that want it.

Her current girlfriend is also named Molly. I don't know
what to think about this terrible coincidence. This other Molly
has annoyed green eyes and cocker spaniel colored hair.
She is a good looking woman with bad manners. Intense and
messy. She'll stare you down if she feels like it. She snubbed
me in public, when we were first introduced. When I mentioned
it to my daughter Molly later, in private, she replied,
"Mother, she treats everybody that way. Even me. She isn't
going to make any exceptions."

Molly says the wrong name scrambled her brain, leaves
her anemic. She calls it her curse. We should have named her
Ignacia, Amonia, Insomnia? Psyche? Vendetta? Asthma?
But it's too late. Thirty years too late.

Cartoons

A huge droopy mouse smacks you on the knee with a rubber
mallet and you zoom up like mercury registering fever. You
hit the top of a tall tree with a loud clang. Your doorbell rings.
It's a fish with a telegram, which blows up in your face the
minute you open it. You're charred black from head to toe.
Then you're fine in the next frame, surrounded by raucous
animal laughter: pigs hee-hee, birds snicker, buck-toothed
horses snort and guffaw. You're the laughing stock, the puny
human who can't gallop or jump high enough. You left your
shoes at school and your clothes at home, stupid. You get
sucked into machines everywhere you go. At the laundromat,
there's your desperate face, orbiting inside the washer's soapy
porthole. When you visit the gym, the machines go haywire.
They whirl and jiggle you almost to death, till, clamped into
the steam machine, you simmer down to the size of a toothpick
and escape. Outside, a stork wings his way across the sky,
dodging puffy clouds, a pastel bundle dangling from his scis-
sory beak. His shadow falls over the flat, asexual landscape,
ominous as a bomber plane's. Moles wearing bifocals poke their
heads up, surfacing through the soft dirt to see what's the
matter. The smart rabbit glaring down the retarded hunter's
gun barrel pauses a moment in his tirade, shades his eyes and
scans the horizon. The cannibals salting you in a pot of hot water
to make soup drop their spoons. Poor you. Poor me. We
lack sufficient lightness to fly up in the coming explosion, then
reassemble. Bogged down by anatomy's mechanical weight,
we'll end up less than sketches. When the mist moves on, if we're
lucky, we'll be part of the earth's enrichment, iotas of loam.
We'll turn into see-through spooks, friendless ghosts without

a note of background music as motif for our movements...
and no audience's hair to raise. The world gone bald, we'll be
spilt spiritual milk, without a glass on the planet left to pour
in to.

The Cure

Just as the doctor promised, I've forgotten a lot. I barely
remember that first place you sent me – those bald, dribbling
women and nurses fat as tubas. Many x-rays later, I'm more of
a glow than a real girl. A radiant skeleton in a billowing gown.
Come take me home. This isn't my place, among odors of
undone laundry and wrung hands. Well, it's September.
They take us for long walks across the safe landscapes. They cut
bouquets for our rooms. When you first arrive, they crop
your hair short. Then the mountain air bites the back of your
neck. The breathing machine makes a great deal of noise, but I
can still sleep. I attend church services on Sunday. I'm not a
believer but I love sitting among them. A sullen man to my right
whose adam's apple jumps convulsively wants to share his
bothersome thoughts with me. Better never to speak to anyone,
to reseed this silence like the echo of lost talk caught in a dead
woman's ear trumpet. He opens his palm and leans over to show
me the little wrinkled map in his hand. His eyes gleam as if he's
been eating uranium. There's no use explaining, crying, knit-
ting or singing. Even this exquisite, vigorous prose you're read-
ing right now isn't mine. It's his. I recognize the handwriting.

The Bishop's Visit

Monks and nuns walk haltingly, carrying trays of chocolate malteds – sweet treats for the bishop and his entourage. A young nun drops her tray, and brown liquid splatters her habit. But she anticipates forgiveness. The monks and nuns in this co-ed cloister shape and color each other's devotion. Together, they contemplate the lessons of childhood. They compare guardian angels.... "Mine had white wings." "Oh, mine apologized twice for being late, said she had a lot of visits to make that day." On the young monk's first night in his cell, his bad dream featured a funeral in paisley green motif. Probably due to overexcitement about the bishop's visit, and an official glimpse at his Eminence's divine life. An existence limited to intellectual pleasures, plus an occasional puff on a cigarette bearing a saintly lady's name. The respected author read a newspaper account of her accident, and felt a sudden inexplicable rush of love for its subject. He *had* to see her. He stood in the doorway of the hospital ward, looking in. The sight haunted his mind for weeks. Finally, he contacted the monastery about a lay-person's retreat, so he could calm his frayed nerves and polish his novel. But the guest room was very drafty. He didn't get much work done. And he suffered from heartburn, as the monks and nuns served him nothing but fish-sticks, reserving all other delicacies they had to offer the bishop.

The Holy Ghost

lives in the clear liquid that flows through the veins of oak leaves. Whether that fluid has been named or not. Known or unknown, visible or just guessed at, the holy ghost is composed of what little light the prisoner sees through the weave of her blindfold. The holy ghost is smoke and melodrama, the orange and pink tongues of fire whiskey drinkers acquire when they hear the whiz of any barmaid's whip, or their dead parents yelling at them. The holy ghost makes his presence known the moment humans tune in to the everpresent din of all objects talking at once: barstools squealing, the worried clink of glasses and sob and slop of spirit—these sounds summon listeners, just as a mother catches her son's eye and points to his pyjamas (like a fisherman beckoning with his net) to indicate to the child he has stayed awake long past his bedtime. So it is that the holy ghost holds his bullhorn, and his several voices ring in our ears worse than our thundering drunken blood does. He orders us to hug everyone else in the bar, saying "those who are by nature lovers are condemned to each other's arms."

CONTENTS

Introduction   8
Christine   11
Since You've Been Gone   12
Drifter   13
Night Sweats   14
Repose   15
Repose   16
I Fall to Pieces   17
Travelogue   18
White Sleep   19
This Winter   21
January   22
Chatterbox   23
Soft Talk   24
Perpetual Honeymoon   25
Lullaby   26
Kindergarten   28
Müttergluck   29
Elementary School   30
V-E Day   31
Berlin   32
Impressions of the Midwest   33
Dry Land   34
This Explains Everything   36
Looking at a Medical Text Containing
    Color Photos of an Autopsy   37
Loomings   38
Slow Boat   39

New Mutiny   41
White Marriage   43
The True Bride   45
Remain Awake   47
Bread and Butter   49
Catherine   51
Alice and Lewis   53
Text for Jeff   55
Martine's Mouth   59
A Lecture on Jealousy   62
Dear Boy George   63
A Letter   64
Molly   65
Cartoons   67
The Cure   69
The Bishop's Visit   70
The Holy Ghost   71

This book was designed and printed at the Lapis Press in Santa Monica, California by Jaime Robles, Les Ferriss and Christopher Stinehour. The text was set in Monotype Bembo by Patrick Reagh; the titles were set in Spectrum italic and Cancelleresca, types designed by Jan van Krimpen.